I0528379

How Eagle, Crow and Turtle Got Their Colors

A Fable

Author/Illustrator

H. N. Henry

Copyright © 2023 by Huard, Norman Henry

All rights reserved. No part of this publication may be reproduced, distributed or transmitted in any form or by any means without prior written permission.

PRESSE DRAGON LIBRE / FREE DRAGON'S PRESS
Huard, Norman Henry
220 B Farmer
Trois-Rivières, Québec, Canada, G9A 3E6
https://hnhenry.com/home/

Editor's note: This is a work of fiction. Names, characters, places and incidents are the product of the author's imagination. Places and public names are sometimes used for atmospheric purposes. Any resemblance to real persons, living or dead, or to businesses, companies, events, institutions or places is entirely coincidental.

How Eagle, Crow and Turtle Got Their Colors / H. N. Henry — 1st edition
ISBN   978-1-998882-21-2   POD

ACKNOWLEDGMENTS

This story is an adaptation of one told by the character, King Godomor, to the heroine, Nagora, in *BRANDED* Book II of The Dragon's Game Series, a six-book fantasy series the author wrote. To learn more about the author and that series, please visit his website.

DEDICATION

To my son, Lennon.

It was a warm spring Sunday afternoon as ten-year-old Nagora walked up to Grandpa's home to visit him and to ask him to tell her a story. She found him outside near his woodpile, sitting cross-legged on a red woolen blanket. He was chopping pencil-thin kindling sticks from a split birch log. She admired his concentration as he swung his hatchet with skill and precision. Without speaking a word, she waited for him to acknowledge her presence. After planting the ax head on the chopping stump, he looked up at her and smiled. "Granddaughter, I am happy to see you. I was expecting you. Come, Nagora. Sit with me. I made sweet tea the way you like it with honey and milk." Pointing to the thermos standing on the blanket beside him, he asked, "Will you drink with me?"

Nagora returned his smile and sat on the blanket. "Yes, please, Grandpa. I am happy to see you."

Grandpa poured tea into the enameled tin cups. He handed the yellow one to Nagora and then picked up the blue one and lifted it to his lips to drink.

Nagora did the same, savoring the sweetness of the tea as she thought about it.

Only Grandpa's tea tastes this good. It's because of the goat's milk and honey.
"Grandpa, your tea is good!"

He nodded in his calm, reflective way. Nagora was eager to ask him to tell her a favorite story. She hadn't heard it in a long time, but she knew to wait for him to give her a sign that she could ask a question, any question.

He set his cup on the chopping stump, placed his hands on his knees, and looked into his granddaughter's eyes. "Nagora wishes to talk today?" he asked.

"I want to listen today. Grandpa, please tell me the story of how eagle, crow and turtle got their colors."

"Nagora, you ask for a good story." His eyes and lips smiled at her, deepening the creases on his weather-worn face. "I will tell it as my far-away great grandfather told it to be passed on to me by my grandfather."

With a sweep of one hand and then the other to show the nearby forest, fields and lakes, he began. "The Land had been white with the snow of Winter for a long, long time, without his sisters Spring, Summer and Fall coming to visit. So long that all the animals in The Land were white.

"The bears were white, the foxes were white, the owls were white, as were all the birds and turtles. It was time for Winter to leave."

Grandpa reached for his cup, looked at Nagora and asked, "How did Winter know it was time to leave?"

Nagora did not answer as she remembered it was Grandpa's way to pause as he told the story and that he would answer the question. Sipping from the still hot tea, she waited while he, too, drank from his cup.

Grandpa set his cup on the chopping stump and pointed at Nagora. "Winter knew because Kaw had given that task to Turtle. Nagora, do you remember who Kaw is?"

Knowing the answer, Nagora smiled. "Yes, Grandpa. 'Kaw' is Sun's nickname."

Grandpa returned her smile and raised a hand, showing the sun in the sky. "When Turtle was very young, long before Winter came for the long stay, Sun instructed Turtle, 'I have a task for you. When you become ancient and white and ready to die, you must remind me to ask Winter to leave The Land.'" Grandpa squinted as his face and his voice became solemn. He pointed at Nagora again.

"'Only you, Turtle, can remind me. If you do not find a way, Winter will stay forever in The Land and keep it covered in snow and ice. Turtle, I am choosing you because you are to be the last of your kind in The Land. Make your ancestors proud as they look down on you from the stars.'" Grandpa crossed his arms and rubbed his shoulders, pretending to shiver.

"Winter stayed in The Land for many years, freezing the long cold days into longer colder nights. Winter covered the forests, plains, lakes and mountains with snow and ice and howling winds.

"During all that time, Turtle lived in a hole at the bottom of the tree where Eagle nested. Turtle survived on scraps of fish that Eagle hunted in the unfrozen parts of the sea."

Grandpa pulled his shirt collar closer around his neck and tapped a finger on the side of his head. "All those long cold nights, Turtle tried to figure out how to remind Sun that it was time for Winter to leave.

"Turtle thought long and hard to find a way. *'I cannot fly to Sun. Only a powerful bird can bring my message to Sun. Will Eagle fly to Sun for me? How will I convince Eagle?'*"

Grandpa joined the tips of his fingers and thumbs high above his head. "One moonlit night, Turtle awoke from a dream. *'I have it! I have what it takes to give Eagle the strength to fly to Sun! Will I be able to convince Eagle?'*"

Grandpa reached for the thermos. "More tea, Nagora?"

She shook her head no. "I still have half a cup. I like how it tastes when it is cold."

He smiled at her and filled his cup. "There is plenty left."

Grandpa set the thermos on the blanket, screwed the cap on, and then reached for his cup. Placing his other hand on the side of the cup, he felt its warmth for a moment. Then he blew on the hot tea before taking two small sips.

After setting his cup down, Grandpa continued. "In the last days of his life, Turtle spoke to Eagle about the important task Kaw had given long ago. 'Eagle, will you fly to Sun to deliver an important message?'" Grandpa crossed his hands, palms up, hooked his thumbs together and flapped his fingers like wings.

Nagora watched the imaginary bird fly as Grandpa spoke.

"At first Eagle said, 'But I do not have the strength to fly that far, and if I did, I could get burned by the fire of Sun.'

"Then Turtle explained how it would be possible. 'Eagle, soon, when I die, you must eat me so my flesh will not become frozen and uneatable. You must empty my shell of all my flesh. If you eat it all, you will have the strength to fly to Sun.'"

Grandpa drew his head back; his eyes opened wide with concern to stare at Nagora. "'I cannot eat you, Turtle! You are my friend!'"

"Turtle replied, 'Eagle, all these years I have eaten scraps from your hunts because Winter froze all my ponds and streams. Eat me as soon as I die, before my flesh freezes, so you can fly somewhere you have never been and deliver an important message.'"

At this part of the story, Grandpa's face and words caused Nagora to bite on her lower lip. Her eyes blinked to hold back her tears. Turtle's talk of death made Nagora feel sad, yet proud, because Turtle had the courage to ask Eagle for help. *Turtle must have great trust in Eagle,* thought Nagora.

"Then Eagle asked, 'What if I burn up before I deliver the message?'"

Grandpa made the motion of pulling something over his head and then hooked a finger on each side of his head next to his eyes. "'You will not, Eagle, because you will wear my shell on your head. You will see out of my leg holes. Your beak will stick out where my head does now.'" As Grandpa pulled on his nose, drawing it out and down like the beak of an eagle, he crossed his eyes, causing Nagora to giggle.

"'You will fill my shell with snow and ice to keep you from burning up.'

"Eagle considered the words of Turtle and weighed the risks. '*There is wisdom in the words of Turtle, but I want to know more.*' And so, Eagle asked, 'What is the message?'

"'My shell is the message. Tell Sun that I send it as a gift. Sun will understand.'

"The answer Turtle gave caused Eagle to ask, 'Why can I not know the message that I will risk my life to deliver?'

"'Eagle, Kaw told me long ago that only I can be the reminder of the message, no one else! But, Eagle, I am sure Sun will share the message with you, and reward you once you deliver my gift!'

"Eagle looked from his friend, Turtle, up to the sky." Grandpa pointed his nose skyward and spread his arms. "Eagle scanned the horizon from one end of The Land, covered in snow, to the other end, along the icy shore of the sea."

Nagora watched Grandpa's slow imitation of Eagle as she sipped the tea and savored its sweet smell until he continued telling the story.

"When Eagle looked back at his friend, he declared, 'Turtle, my old friend, I sense the urgency and importance of your message to Kaw. I will deliver your shell to help you, not for the reward, but for the challenge to fly further and higher than ever before.'"

Grandpa reached for his cup and took a sip. He winked at Nagora as he raised the index finger of his other hand. Pointing to his ear, he shifted his eyes toward it. "Now, all the while, Crow was hiding under a snow-covered bush, listening to all of this. Crow said to himself, '*I will not miss out on this. There is a reward. I want part of it. I will watch and wait and follow Eagle, just as I always do to get the best scraps.*'"

"When the time of death came for Turtle, he called to Eagle, and Eagle kept his promise." Grandpa made the motion of pulling something over his head.

"Eagle put on the shell of Turtle and filled it with snow and pieces of ice. It was heavy, but Eagle felt stronger than ever before."

Grandpa held his arms out at his sides and moved them up and down. "Eagle spread his strong wings wide to fly toward Sun."

Again, Grandpa made the bird with his hands, and again, Nagora followed it as Grandpa spoke. "Before long, Eagle heard Crow call from behind.

"'It is too far to fly! We will never get there!'"

"Eagle ignored Crow." Grandpa waved a hand over his shoulder in dismissal.

"Then Eagle heard Crow complain again. 'It is too hot! I am thirsty!'"

"Eagle pretended not to hear Crow." Again, Grandpa waved his hand.

"The melting snow and ice from inside the shell of Turtle refreshed Eagle. The strong wings of Eagle kept up their steady beat, bringing Eagle closer to Sun with each powerful flap."

Grandpa's eyes opened wide in surprise. "Crow bit onto the tail of Eagle!"

Nagora smiled as she saw the scene play out in her mind.

Grandpa spread his arms wide and shook his shoulders back and forth. "Eagle tried to shake off Crow."

"Eagle yelled at Crow. 'Let go of my tail!'" Grandpa swept his hands back at his sides, shaking them as if sweeping something off his back.

"Crow did not let go. He knew that if he did, he could never keep up on his own. At least now, a few drops of water from the melting snow in the shell of Turtle found their way to the mouth of Crow. They helped lessen his thirst, allowing him to keep holding on to the tail of Eagle. Eagle paid no attention to Crow, hoping the heat of Kaw would make Crow let go as they flew closer and closer. But no, Crow did not let go. *I want part of the reward. I did not come this far to just let go. We are almost there and I will get a share of the reward,*' said Crow to himself."

Grandpa cupped a hand next to his mouth. "Sun called out, 'Who comes my way?'" Grandpa cupped his other hand to the other side of his mouth.

"Eagle answered, 'It is Eagle. I bring a gift from Turtle.'"

Grandpa expanded his chest and made the come forward motion with his open hands. "'Come closer,' Sun said. 'I will not harm you.'"

"Eagle flew closer and spoke. 'Sun, here is the shell of my friend, Turtle.'" Grandpa made the bird and brought his hands to the side of his head, removing the imaginary shell.

"To Eagle, Sun replied, 'I see! The shell of your friend, Turtle, is reminding me it is time for me to speak to Winter. I will tell Winter to leave The Land. The People of The Land will decide what to do. I will reward Turtle. Turtle will not be the last of his kind in The Land. Turtle will have brothers and sisters, and wherever they are, they will have shells with patterns and colors that will please all eyes.

"'Eagle, as the messenger of Turtle, I will reward you.'"

Grandpa squinted and pointed, pretending to look behind Nagora. "'Eagle, what is that on your tail?' asked Sun.

"At that moment, Crow let go of the tail of Eagle. 'It is I, Crow! I helped Eagle bring the message of Turtle!'

"'Is that so, Eagle?' asked Sun."

Grandpa shook his head no. "'Crow lies. He always follows me around for scraps. Crow must want part of the reward.'

"'Well Crow, if that is so, I will reward you too!' said Sun.

"The prospect of also getting a reward made the beak of Crow hang open.

"Sun proclaimed, 'First, Crow, with my heat. Before you leave here, I will not leave a speck of white on you. I will burn you black, and all your brothers and sisters as well, wherever they are. All of you will have black feathers, black beaks and black claws.

"'Second, Crow, with a song. From now on, you and all your brothers and sisters will sing my nickname whenever you speak.'"

Grandpa cupped his hands to his mouth. "'Kaw! Kaw! Kaw!' was all Crow could manage, such was his dismay."

Grandpa waved his finger as if scolding. "'That will do, Crow! From now on, your color and your song will announce your arrival wherever you go.

"'Eagle, for helping Turtle, I give you and all your brothers and sisters, wherever they are, beaks of gold and talons of gold. They will complement your feathers that have darkened on your long flight to me. In memory of your friendship with Turtle, you may keep your head of white.

"'And, because Crow will continue to follow you, keep your tail of white to remind him of the color he once was.

"'Return to The Land and let The People know Winter will leave and return only once a year from now on.'

"Eagle and Crow returned to The Land, and when The People saw their new colors, they believed the message of Eagle and made their choices.

"Some of the young and strong followed Winter to continue to live with him as they continued to adapt to life surrounded by snow, ice and cold.

"Some of the young and strong stayed behind to care for the elders and the sick, who were too weak to take the journey to Winter.

"The People who stayed looked forward to live in The Land where sisters Spring, Summer and Fall would come to visit each year. They would help The People provision for that time of year when brother Winter would come again."

With a smile, Grandpa clasped his hands on one bent knee and leaned back as he looked at Nagora.

Nagora looked back at him, returning his smile. "Grandpa, this story makes my heart happy. It is a good story to hear. It is one of my favorites. I will remember it always. It is a precious gift I will carry in my heart."

Grandpa smiled and reached for his thermos. "And you will tell it to others."

As Nagora nodded, she crossed her hands palms up, hooked her thumbs, and flapped her fingers like wings.

As Grandpa watched her bird fly skyward, his smile broadened. "More tea, Granddaughter?"

"Yes, please, Grandpa!"

ABOUT THE AUTHOR

Norm taught grade 1 children for ten years, and reader's and writer's workshop and visual arts in high school for sixteen years. Those experiences and having written a six-book fantasy series have given him a true appreciation of how people, young and old, are wired to love stories.

Forever on the lookout for eagles while sea kayaking and sailing, Norm finds inspiration on coastal waters and lakes for the stories he writes, like this fable.

His studies of stained-glass window design, cartoon animation, past and contemporary art styles have definitely influenced the digital illustrations in this book.

He shares the profits from his work with a local community cause, Point de Rue. They help homeless people find meaning and passion in their lives.

To connect with the author, please visit his website: https://hnhenry.com/home/.

Dear Reader,

Your voice truly matters. If you enjoyed reading and discussing this fable with your child, or with your students, and think that other parents and teachers would too, it would mean the world to me if you would take a minute to leave a heartfelt review on Amazon. Doing so helps other parents and teachers choose worthwhile books to share with their kids.

Also, I truly appreciate your kind feedback. It is so very important. It helps me continue to grow as a writer and storyteller.

Thank you for your time.

H. N. Henry

https://hnhenry.com/home/review-page_book_gtc/

Looking for the
Companion Coloring Book
How Eagle, Crow and Turtle Got Their
Colors?

This ISBN: 978-1-998882-29-8 will help
you find it wherever you buy books.

There's an <u>audio-book</u> version too!

To purchase these online, follow this
link or the QR Code below.
https://hnhenry.com/home/how-eagle-
crow-and-turtle-got-their-colors/

www.ingramcontent.com/pod-product-compliance
Lightning Source LLC
Chambersburg PA
CBHW041731140626
46547CB00025BA/292